IRAQ
the people

April Fast

A Bobbie Kalman Book
The Lands, Peoples, and Cultures Series

 Crabtree Publishing Company
www.crabtreebooks.com

The Lands, Peoples, and Cultures Series

Created by Bobbie Kalman

Author: April Fast

Third edition: Q2AMedia

Editor: Adrianna Morganelli

Content and Photo editor: Kokila Manchanda

Editorial director: Kathy Middleton

Production coordinator: Margaret Salter

Prepress technician: Margaret Salter

Project manager: Kumar Kanul

First and second editions
  Coordinating editor: Ellen Rodger
  Project editor: Rachel Eagen
  Production coordinator: Rosie Gowsell
  Project development: First Folio Resource Group, Inc.
  Photo research: Maria DeCambra
  Consultants: Thabit Abdullah, Department of History, York University; Majid Aziza

Cover: A woman prepares wool for knitting a carpet in Baghdad's Sadr city.

Title page: A young man carefully balances a platter of breads covered with sesame seeds on his head.

Icon: The Ma'dan, or Marsh Arabs, live in Iraq's southern marshlands. They traditionally use the marshes' reeds to build homes with columns, arches, and vaulted roofs.

Back cover: Carp swim in almost every stream, river, and lake in Iraq, and they are raised on fish farms. Most carp caught in Iraq are eaten locally.

Photographs
AFP: Ahmad Al- Rubaye p. 5 (top); Sabah Arar: p. 26 (bottom)
AP Photo: CP/Laurent Rebours: p. 17; Ali Haider: p. 18 (top), p. 29; Jassim Mohammed: p. 31 (left); Alexander Zemlianichenko: p. 21 (right)
Art Archive: Musée du Louvre Paris/Dagli Orti: p. 7 (right), p. 30 (bottom)
Art Directors: Ask Images: p. 25 (bottom); Jane Sweeney: p. 10 (left), p. 27 (right), p. 31 (right);
Associated Media Group: Peter Langer: title page, p. 25 (top)
Atlas Geographic: Fatih Pinar: p. 20 (left)
British Museum, London, UK: Bridgeman Art Library: p. 6, p. 10 (right); Ancient Art and Architecture Collection Ltd./Bridgeman Art Library: p. 8 (top)
Corbis: Maher Attar/Magma: p. 23; Bettmann/Magma: p. 11 (left), p. 13 (right); Magma: p. 12 (left), p. 16 (left); Gianni Dagli Orti/Magma: p. 7 (left); Araldo de Luca/Magma: p. 9; Liz Hafalia/San Francisco Chronicle/Magma: p. 21 (left); Thomas Hartwell/Magma: p. 4 (right); Hulton-Deutsch Collection/Magma: p. 12 (right), p. 13 (left); Charles & Josette Lenars/Magma: p. 3, p. 8 (bottom); Michael Macor/San Francisco Chronicle/Magma: p. 24 (bottom); Jehad Nga/Magma: p. 30 (top); Jacques Pavlovsky/Magma: p. 15; Patrick Robert/Magma: p. 16 (right); David Turnley/Magma: p. 26 (top right); Michael S. Yamashita/Magma: p. 28 (right); Dean Conger: p. 19 (left); Michel Setboun: p. 19 (right); Michael S. Yamashita: p. 22
CP/Ron Cortes/KRT/ABACA: p. 24 (top)
Getty Images: Joseph Barrak/AFP: p. 20 (right); Central Press: p. 14; General Photographic Agency: p. 11 (right); Mario Tama: p. 4 (left)
Ivy Images: Nik Wheeler: p. 5 (bottom), p. 27 (left)
Photolibrary: Richard Ashworth: p. 18 (bottom)
Reuters: Kareem Raheem: cover; Nuhad Hussin: p. 28 (top)

Illustrations
Dianne Eastman: icon
David Wysotski, Allure Illustrations: back cover

Library and Archives Canada Cataloguing in Publication

Fast, April, 1968-
    Iraq : the people / April Fast. -- Rev. ed.

(Lands, peoples, and cultures series)
Includes index.
ISBN 978-0-7787-9280-2 (bound).--ISBN 978-0-7787-9650-3 (pbk.)

    1. Iraq--Social conditions--Juvenile literature.
I. Title. II. Series: Lands, peoples, and cultures series

HN670.A8F38 2010   j956.7   C2009-905131-1

Library of Congress Cataloging-in-Publication Data

Fast, April, 1968-
    Iraq, the people / April Fast. -- Rev. ed.
        p. cm. -- (The lands, peoples, and cultures series)
    "A Bobbie Kalman Book."
    Includes index.
    ISBN 978-0-7787-9650-3 (pbk. : alk. paper) -- ISBN 978-0-7787-9280-2 (reinforced library binding : alk. paper)
    1. Iraq--Juvenile literature. I. Title. II. Series.

DS70.62.F37 2010
956.7--dc22

2009034654

Crabtree Publishing Company

www.crabtreebooks.com   1-800-387-7650

Printed in China/122009/CT20090915

Published in Canada
Crabtree Publishing
616 Welland Ave.
St. Catharines, ON
L2M 5V6

Published in the United States
Crabtree Publishing
350 Fifth Ave.,
59th Floor
New York, NY 10118

Published in the United Kingdom
Crabtree Publishing
Maritime House
Basin Road North, Hove
BN41 1WR

Published in Australia
Crabtree Publishing
386 Mt. Alexander Rd.
Ascot Vale (Melbourne)
VIC 3032

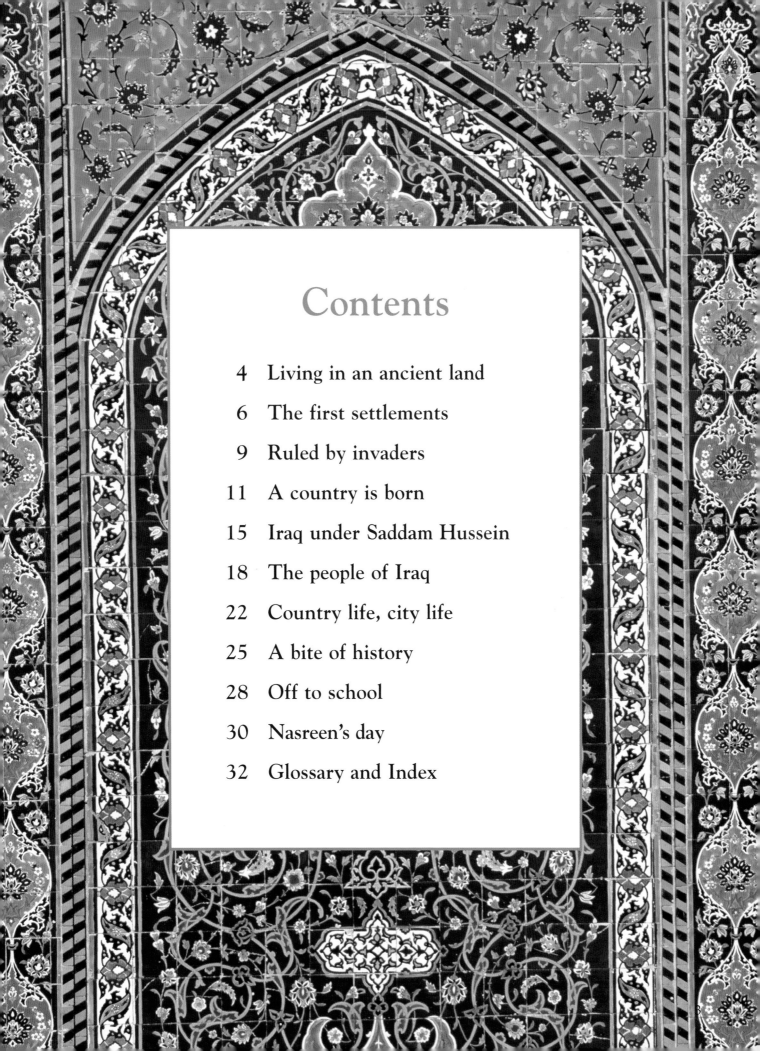

Contents

A Kurdish girl wears brightly colored clothing and a headdress to a traditional wedding celebration.

An ethnic mix

Many peoples from different **ethnic** and religious backgrounds came together when the country of Iraq was formed. Most people were Arabs who followed the religion of **Islam**. There was also a large group of Kurds who lived in the mountains of the north. They followed Islam, too. Communities of Christians, Mandaeans, and others were also part of the new country. Over time, these peoples came together to create a united country, despite periods of tension between groups.

The country of Iraq was created in 1921, but people have lived on this ancient land for tens of thousands of years. Iraq lies in the area known as the Middle East, which borders the southern and eastern shores of the Mediterranean Sea. The country's two main rivers, the Tigris and Euphrates, have long provided the people living there with water for transportation, fishing, farming, and everyday living.

Many civilizations built cities on the banks of the Tigris and Euphrates. Some cities were destroyed by invading armies, while others were abandoned and buried by floods and sandstorms. New cities were built around and even on top of the cities that came before them. These newer cities are where the people of Iraq live today.

Crowds of people shop at a busy street market in Baghdad, where goods such as spices, rugs, jewelry, copperware, and antiques are sold.

Life in Iraq

Iraq's people have suffered harsh treatment from governments they opposed, and they have endured wars with their neighbors and other countries. These wars have devastated the country with **economic** hardships and loss of lives.

In the midst of a turbulent past and an unknown future, the people of Iraq strive to maintain stability in their cities and countryside. Community and family define Iraqis' lives and help bring together the people of this historic land.

(above) The Ma'dan, or Marsh Arabs, travel through their villages in boats made of tall grasses called reeds.

(top) This man heads to the mosque, a Muslim house of worship, to pray. Muslims pray five times a day: before sunrise, in the early afternoon, in the late afternoon, after sunset, and at night.

This wooden panel, made with shells and a stone called lapis lazuli, depicts life in the ancient Sumerian kingdom, including a royal banquet and servants carrying gifts of livestock and fish to the king.

The area now known as Iraq was once called Mesopotamia, which means "land between the rivers" in Greek. People in this region, which lay between the Tigris and Euphrates rivers, built ships, used wheeled wagons and carts, invented writing, and made discoveries in medicine, science, and mathematics that are still important today.

Toward settlement

About 10,000 years ago, nomadic peoples traveled with their animals through Mesopotamia, searching for food and water. They began setting up permanent villages in the northern foothills. Several families lived together in the villages, growing crops and raising livestock. In clay ovens, they baked bread, fired pottery, and made tools, which they traded with traveling merchants for metals and precious stones.

Sumerians

Sumerians settled in southern Mesopotamia around 3500 B.C., in a region that became known as Sumer. They established the first cities along the Tigris and Euphrates. Soon, the cities grew into larger areas called city-states, which included neighboring towns, farmlands, and palm groves. Kings ruled each city-state and often tried to take over other kings' territory.

Most Sumerians farmed, fished, raised livestock, and harvested date palms. Skilled craftspeople made sculptures and pottery, wove textiles, made baskets out of tall grasses called reeds, and built ships. To help them with their work, Sumerians invented the wheeled cart, the potter's wheel, and other tools. They also developed a counting system, a calendar, and the first form of writing, called cuneiform. Symbols and patterns were made by pressing a reed with a wedge-shaped tip into clay. Sumerians also developed cylinder seals to sign documents and mark personal property. Cylinder seals were long, narrow stones with patterns carved into them. They left a distinctive pattern when rolled over clay.

Akkadians

The Akkadians lived north of the Sumerians. Their capital was the city of Akkad, or Agade. Around 2300 B.C., the Akkadian ruler King Sargon I conquered most of Sumer and brought many city-states under his rule. His **dynasty** lasted until about 2200 B.C., when it was weakened because of war. The Akkadian **Empire** fell and, for the next hundred years, various peoples struggled for control of the land.

The return of Sumerian rule

In 2100 B.C., Ur-Nammu, king of the Sumerian city Ur, gained power over southern Mesopotamia. The rules he established for his kingdom became one of the world's earliest collections of laws, known today as the Code of Ur-Nammu. After Ur-Nammu died, his **descendants** expanded his empire. Their rule became known as the Third Dynasty of Ur. Over time, the dynasty began to lose power, and the land was split into four kingdoms. The rulers of those kingdoms fought with one another for control of the land.

Stone reliefs from the Hittite period depicted scenes from everyday life. In this relief, two people play with a spinning top.

King Hammurabi's laws, which became known as the Code of Hammurabi, were carved on stones and placed in temples throughout Babylonia.

Babylonians

The four kingdoms of southern Mesopotamia were unified once again in 1792 B.C. by the Babylonian king Hammurabi. He made the city of Babylon the capital of his empire, Babylonia, which extended north to the region of Assyria. Hammurabi organized great construction projects, including temples, city walls, public buildings, and **canals**, which are manmade waterways. He also created his own set of laws based on those of Ur-Nammu. The Babylonian Empire remained strong until Hammurabi died in 1750 B.C.

Hittites and Kassites

In 1595 B.C., Babylonia was raided by the Hittites, a people from Anatolia, the land that is now eastern Turkey. Around 1500 B.C., the Kassites gained control. The Kassites, who are thought to have come from the mountains east of Babylonia, ruled for about 400 years. During their reign, much of Babylonia was divided into large estates that the king gave to his most loyal supporters. The boundaries of the estates were recorded on large stones called *kudurrus*, along with images of the gods who watched over the land.

The Assyrian Empire

Assyria was an empire in northern Mesopotamia that reached the height of its power in 883 B.C. During that time, kings such as Sargon II and Ashurbanipal sent out armies to conquer new lands. Eventually, the Assyrian Empire stretched from the Persian Gulf in the east to Egypt and Palestine in the west. The great Assyrian Empire came to an end in 612 B.C. when the Medes, who lived in present-day Iran, and the Chaldeans, a Babylonian people, fought each other for control of the land. The main cities of the Assyrian Empire were destroyed in these battles.

The Chaldean Empire

King Nebuchadnezzar II, who ruled from 605 to 562 B.C., was the most famous Chaldean king. In his capital of Babylon, he built an enormous palace that was protected by the Ishtar Gate, named for the Babylonian goddess of **fertility**, love, and war. He also built the Hanging Gardens of Babylon on the ledges of a **ziggurat**. Plants and trees from all parts of his empire were planted on the outer ledges of the terraced ziggurat, creating multileveled rooftop gardens. The gardens were planted for the king's wife, who was homesick for the mountains and greenery of her homeland, Media.

The Assyrians were known as vicious warriors. Their battles were carved in stone reliefs that decorated palaces in their main cities, such as Nimrud and Nineveh.

Under the rule of King Nebuchadnezzar II, Babylon became the site of new temples and palaces, such as the Palace of Nebuchadnezzar.

🏛 Ruled by invaders 🏛

After the Chaldean Empire fell, many different peoples ruled Mesopotamia over the years. In 539 B.C., the armies of Persian ruler Cyrus the Great captured Babylonia. Persia, which is now Iran, was the land east of Mesopotamia.

The conquest was peaceful, and Cyrus the Great treated the people in his new land well. He rebuilt cities that had been destroyed earlier, and Babylonia became the wealthiest province in his empire. However, Persian kings who ruled after Cyrus the Great were harsher and more destructive. The people started to rebel, and the Persian Empire began to lose power.

Alexander the Great

In 331 B.C., Alexander the Great took advantage of Persia's weakening rule and conquered the area. Alexander the Great was the leader of Macedonia, an ancient kingdom of northern Greece. He wanted to restore Babylonia's temples and make the region a center for trade by improving canals and establishing trade routes across his lands, from India in the east to Egypt in the west. Alexander did not fully accomplish his goals before he died of illness at age 32, but he did improve trade and rebuild many of Babylon's historic buildings.

(top) Alexander the Great's empire stretched from Greece to India. He spread Greek ideas and the Greek way of life in the areas he conquered.

Parthians and Sassanians

Those who led after Alexander the Great were not effective rulers, and were conquered by the Parthians around 126 B.C. The Parthians were excellent warriors from Turkestan and other parts of central Asia. They ruled for most of the next 300 years, but were eventually overtaken by the Sassanians, who came from Persia in 224 A.D.

Arab rule

In 633 A.D., Arab followers of Muhammad, the last **Muslim prophet**, began to move across Mesopotamia, spreading their religion, Islam, as they conquered new lands. They toppled the Sassanians in 637 A.D. One of the greatest Muslim caliphs, or religious and political leaders, was Abu Ja'far al-Mansur. He belonged to a branch of Muhammad's family known as the Abassids. A ruler from 754 A.D. to 775 A.D., he built the city of Baghdad on the site of an old village and made it the capital of his empire. It became a center of trade, culture, education, and religion for the next 500 years.

When Tamerlane's armies captured Baghdad, he had his soldiers each cut off two people's heads, which were then arranged to form towers of skulls.

The Mongols

The Abbasid dynasty came to an end in 1258 A.D. The Mongols, a tribe from central Asia, invaded and gained control of Baghdad. The Mongols killed many citizens, including the caliph and his family, and destroyed Baghdad. Once they had control of the city, they settled in the area and partially rebuilt what they had ruined. The Mongols ruled the land for 150 years before the army of Tamerlane, another leader from central Asia, conquered Baghdad in 1401 and destroyed the city once again.

The Ottoman Empire

Tamerlane's rule lasted only a few years. During the period that followed, Turkmen tribes from central Asia fought for control of the area, but no ruler took over the entire region. This changed in 1534, when Mesopotamia became part of the Turkish Ottoman Empire. The Ottoman Empire was based in Constantinople, which is present-day Istanbul, in Turkey. The Ottomans lowered taxes, improved roads, and brought stability to Mesopotamia. Trade increased, cities prospered, and new cities were established.

This shrine near the city of Najaf in southcentral Iraq was built by the Seljuk Turks, who invaded the land in 1055.

During World War I (1914–1918), Great Britain and Germany were enemies. The British feared that the Ottomans, who still ruled Mesopotamia and who sided with the Germans, would take control of the oil fields and **refineries** that the British had developed. To protect their interests in the country, the British sent troops to occupy, or take control of, Mesopotamia. By the end of World War I, they controlled the whole region.

A British mandate

The League of Nations, which was later replaced by the United Nations (UN), was a group of countries that worked together to create world peace. In 1920, the League of Nations mandated Mesopotamia to the British. The British were to rule the land until Mesopotamia, now known as Iraq, could set up a government and become an independent country. Many Iraqis resented outside control and, during the summer of 1920, they took up arms against the British. Their rebellion was harshly suppressed.

More than 170,000 British troops traveled up the Tigris River as they advanced on Baghdad in 1915, during World War I.

Great Britain and Germany set their sights on Mesopotamia in the late 1800s. The British wanted the land so they could travel through it to their territory in India. They also wanted to dig for oil in Mesopotamia. Germans wanted to build a railway from their capital, Berlin, straight to Baghdad, which had become an important trading center.

The Mesopotomian Commission, which included British prime minister Winston Churchill, was set up after World War I to discuss the future of Mesopotamia.

11

Faisal I

In 1921, fearing another rebellion, the British agreed to set up an Iraqi parliament. This government would consist of a king, a prime minister, and a group of elected and appointed representatives. Britain, however, would still control the country's armed forces and police, as well as hold decision-making power.

The British crowned Faisal, a man from a prominent family in what is now Saudi Arabia, king of Iraq. Iraqis were unhappy that a non-Iraqi was made king of their land. Some were also frustrated by the fact that Faisal belonged to the Sunni branch of Islam, when most Iraqis belonged to the Shi'i branch of Islam. These two branches had developed after Muhammad died. King Faisal faced the difficult task of uniting peoples from different religious and ethnic backgrounds in a land foreign to him, while trying to gain their loyalty.

Faisal I was king of Syria before he became the Iraqi king in 1921.

In a treaty signed in 1930, known as the Anglo-Iraqi treaty, Britain promised to recognize Iraq as an independent country.

Toward independence

Iraqis continued to struggle under British rule, and in 1932, Great Britain granted Iraq independence. The country was officially recognized as an independent state and member of the League of Nations on October 3, 1932. Great Britain still held influence over Iraq's **natural resources** and relations with foreign lands. **Treaties** signed earlier, including one in which Iraq promised to support Great Britain in times of war, also tied the two countries together.

King Ghazi

King Faisal ruled until his death in 1933. His son, Ghazi, became the next king. King Ghazi's rule was marked by political instability, including military **coups**.

When King Ghazi died in a car accident in April 1939, his four-year-old son, Faisal II, became king. Faisal II was too young to rule the country, so his uncle Abd al-Ilah ruled in his place. Members of the Iraqi government thought that Abd al-Ilah was more concerned with British interests than Iraqi interests, and in 1940, they forced him to leave the country.

World War II

During World War II (1939–1945), Great Britain wanted to move its troops across Iraq and store supplies in the country. Iraq refused to grant permission, breaking the terms of a treaty signed in 1930. In April 1941, fighting broke out between Iraqi and British troops, and in May, the British occupied Baghdad. They put Abd al-Ilah back in power and set up a pro-British government.

Revolution

During and after World War II, life in Iraq was marked by food shortages, unemployment, high prices, and limited freedom of speech. Many Iraqis were unhappy and wanted political change. Young military leaders formed a group called the Free Officers and overthrew the government on July 14, 1958. Members of the royal family, including King Faisal II and Abd al-Ilah, were killed. The leader of the revolution, Abd al-Karim Qasim, promised the people a new era of freedom, genuine independence, and a government elected by the people, with a president and officials who would work on behalf of all Iraqis. Qasim was appointed prime minister of this new system of government, known as a republic.

Despite instability during his rule, King Ghazi managed to make improvements within the country. He built new canals, oil pipelines, and schools, and he boosted foreign trade.

The Ba'th Party takes power

Even though Iraq had been declared a republic, the military controlled the government. In 1963, a branch of the army, along with a group of **activists** called the Arab Ba'th **Socialist** Party, overthrew the government. The Arab Ba'th Socialist Party disagreed with Qasim's goal of building Iraq's strength as an independent nation. Instead, it believed that all Arab countries in the Middle East, including Iraq, should form one Arab state based on socialist principles. Qasim was killed, and thousands more were arrested and executed, or put to death, in the fighting.

The Ba'th Party named Abd al-Salam Arif Iraq's new president. He had led the Free Officers' march in 1958. Later that year, Arif removed the Ba'thists from the government, even though they had placed him in power. When he was killed in an accident three years later, his brother, Abd al-Rahman Arif, was chosen as the new president.

A rebel soldier stands on the lawn of the royal palace, examining the looting that took place during the 1958 revolution, when the royal family was killed.

Saddam Hussein

The Ba'th Party rebuilt itself from 1963 to 1968, focusing on creating a strong military division. The Ba'thists overthrew Abd al-Rahman Arif's government on July 17, 1968, and Ahmad Hassan al-Bakr became the president of the Ba'th government.

One of al-Bakr's most loyal assistants was a man named Saddam Hussein. Hussein rose quickly in the ranks of the Ba'th Party and became deputy chairman, the second most powerful position in Iraq. He helped Iraq's government take control of the country's oil operations, which were being run by British and other foreign companies. Iraqis' taxes were lowered, their salaries were increased, and education improved. Hussein led campaigns to eliminate **illiteracy**, and he encouraged equal pay and equal job opportunities for women. When President al-Bakr announced his resignation on July 16, 1979, Saddam Hussein became president.

Keeping control

To assert his power and frighten off anyone who might challenge his rule, Hussein had many political rivals and enemies executed in the first days of his presidency. He also encouraged citizens to spy on friends and neighbors. Anyone suspected of working against the Ba'th government, or even speaking out against its policies, was reported to the government. The "spies" were rewarded and the people they caught were imprisoned, beaten, or even killed. In time, no one dared speak out against Hussein or his government.

In 1970, Saddam Hussein met with Mullah Mustafa Barazani, a Kurdish religious leader, to announce that the Iraqi government would recognize the Kurds as a "national group" and allow self-rule in an area of northern and northeastern Iraq. In 1974, war broke out when the Kurds did not agree to the boundaries of the region because an area rich in oil was left out. The war continued until the Iranians, who were supplying the Kurds with weapons, food, and money, stopped supporting them.

Iraq under Saddam Hussein

In the late 1970s, the new leader of Iran, Iraq's neighbor to the east, began speaking out against Saddam Hussein. Iran and Iraq had struggled in the past for control of one another's land. Iran's leader Ayatollah Khomeini also disliked Iraq's Ba'thist government because it did not practice the strict Muslim faith that Khomeini demanded in Iran. Khomeini broadcasted messages urging Iraqis to remove Hussein from power, and he tried to have several Ba'th officials killed.

The Iran-Iraq War
In 1980, Saddam Hussein began a war against Iran known as the Iran-Iraq War. The war lasted eight years, until 1988, when Hussein launched a massive missile attack against Iran's major cities. He had received weapons and financial support from France, the former Soviet Union, and the United States. Finally, Iran agreed to a **cease-fire**, and the war ended a month later, in August 1988.

Fighting the Kurds
After the Iran-Iraq War, Saddam Hussein turned on the Kurds, many of whom had sided with the Iranians during the war because of their own disputes with the Iraqi government. Hussein's warplanes and helicopters released chemical weapons, which included gases and other harmful substances, that contaminated the water and air above Kurdish villages. About 100,000 Kurds fled to Turkey and Iran to avoid the deadly chemicals. Others were captured by Iraqi forces, and were either killed or sent to concentration camps. The camps were like prisons, where large groups of people were denied food and water and were frequently beaten. Hussein's army destroyed more than 90 percent of the Kurdish villages before he declared victory.

(top) The Iran-Iraq War cost each country about $100 billion and 500,000 lives.

The Persian Gulf War

For many years, Iraq had argued with Kuwait, its neighbor to the south, over land boundaries. Iraq had also accused Kuwait of producing too much oil. This drove down the price of oil on the world market and lowered the **profits** of oil-producing countries. On August 2, 1990, Iraq invaded Kuwait, beginning the Persian Gulf War. Iraq's army of 100,000 soldiers and 300 tanks was much larger than Kuwait's. The Kuwaiti army surrendered and its emir, or ruler, fled the country.

When Saddam Hussein did not pull his troops out of Kuwait, the United Nations called for economic sanctions against Iraq. These sanctions, or restrictions, prevented members of the UN from sending food, weapons, or supplies to Iraq, and from buying its oil. The UN hoped that, without money from oil sales, Iraq would be unable to produce weapons and would be forced to withdraw from Kuwait.

On January 17, 1991, with Iraqi troops still in Kuwait, a **coalition** of 28 nations, including many Arab countries, began a missile assault on Iraq. The attacks were called Operation Desert Storm. On February 24, 1991, the **allied** forces marched into Kuwait. Within two days, they had forced the Iraqi army to retreat. Operation Desert Storm ended on February 28, 1991.

Generals from the United States, Saudi Arabia, and Iraq discuss the conditions of a cease-fire during the last months of Operation Desert Storm.

Kurdish refugees fled from Iraqi forces through the mountains to reach the safety of Turkey.

The Kurds and Shi'is rebel

After the Persian Gulf War, Hussein used his army to stop rebellions in the north and south. Shia Muslims living in southern Iraq were struggling for more influence in government decisions. Kurds living in the north were fighting for the right to rule themselves.

As a result of the fighting, thousands of Shia and Kurds died. Around 250,000 Shia of Persian descent were either forced to leave the country or they fled to Iran, and hundreds of thousands of Kurdish **refugees** went to Turkey. In addition, more than 600,000 Kurds and Shia sought shelter in refugee camps set up by British, Iranian, French, and American troops in northern and southern Iraq. The troops also established no-fly zones in the north and south that prevented planes from flying in those areas. Kurds and Shia no longer had to fear Iraqi fighter planes dropping bombs from above.

After the war

After years of war and economic sanctions, Iraqis did not have enough food or medicine to survive. In 1995, the UN launched the Oil-for-Food program. This program allowed Iraqis to sell small amounts of oil so that it could purchase food and medicine. In return, Iraqis agreed to destroy all its chemical, **biological**, and **nuclear** weapons, under the supervision of UN weapons inspectors.

Not all the money from oil sales went to Iraqis most in need; much of it went to Ba'thist supporters. In addition, the government refused to let UN inspectors examine weapons facilities. In October 1998, Saddam Hussein demanded that all inspectors leave Iraq.

9/11 and its aftermath

On September 11, 2001, **terrorists** from a **radical** Muslim group called Al-Qaeda attacked cities in the United States. They hijacked airplanes and crashed them into the Pentagon, near Washington, DC, and the World Trade Center in New York City. Another hijacked plane crashed in Pennsylvania. Thousands of people were killed and many more were injured.

The U.S. government expressed concern that Saddam Hussein was hiding terrorists and supplying them with weapons. The United States also feared that Hussein's government was manufacturing chemical and nuclear weapons.

Due to increased pressure from the United States and fearing military action, Hussein allowed weapons inspectors to re-enter Iraq in 2002. No chemical or nuclear weapons were found. The United States still worried that Saddam Hussein was a threat to American safety, so it demanded that Hussein leave his country. When he refused, the U.S. led allied troops in an attack on Iraq in March 2003. Hussein went into hiding. American troops did not find him until December 13, 2003, when they discovered him in a hole near Tikrit, the town where he was born.

After Hussein's fall

Many Iraqis celebrated the end of Hussein's harsh rule, but his supporters attacked coalition forces that had stayed in the country until Iraqis could organize a new government. An interim government was established in June 2004, made up of individuals chosen by the Iraqi Governing Council and the Coalitional Provisional Authority (CPA). The CPA was established by the U.S.-led coalition. Then, in January 2005, Iraqis voted for a Transitional National Assembly. This was followed by the parliamentary elections of December 2005 and finally, the formation of an Iraqi government under Prime Minister Jawad al-Maliki in April 2006. As Iraq looks forward to the next parliamentary elections of May 2010, U.S. President Obama has announced the withdrawal of U.S. troops from Iraq and the handing over of security duties to the Iraqi forces to be completed by the end of 2011.

Iraqis pull down a statue of Saddam Hussein in Baghdad on April 9, 2003.

Muslims say special prayers on Friday, the holiest day of the week according to Islam.

Iraq is home to Arabs, who make up about 80 percent of the population; Kurds, who make up about 15 percent of the population; and Assyrians, Turkmen, and Armenians, who make up about five percent of the population. Other small ethnic groups, such as Persians and Mandaeans, live throughout the country.

Arabs

Iraqi Arabs are descended from the Arabs who conquered the land in 637 A.D. Most are Muslims, or people who follow the religion of Islam. Muslims believe in one God, whose name in Arabic is Allah, and follow the teachings of his prophets, the last of whom was Muhammad.

Iraq's Muslims belong to one of two main groups: Shi'i or Sunni. The two groups developed after Muhammad died in 632 A.D. Sunnis believed that future caliphs should be chosen from among Muhammad's followers, while Shia believed the religious and political leaders should be descendants of Muhammad's cousin and son-in-law, Ali. Both groups follow the *Qur'an*, the Muslim holy book, which contains the teachings of Allah, but they developed different codes of behavior, called *Sunna*.

18

Marsh Arabs

The land where the Tigris and Euphrates meet, in southern Iraq, is covered in marshes that are home to a semi nomadic people called the Ma'dan. The Ma'dan, who are also known as Marsh Arabs, are believed to have descended from the Sumerians who lived in the area 6,000 years ago. Their main sources of livelihood are herding water buffalo, hunting waterfowl, and fishing from canoes made from the marshes' reeds.

During the Iran-Iraq War, soldiers fleeing forced military service and others escaping **persecution** hid in the marshlands. The government began draining the marshes to drive the rebels out of their hiding spots. The marshlands are now only seven percent of their original size. Most Marsh Arabs were forcedto leave their traditional way of life and move to other parts of Iraq and to Iran. Today, environmental groups are attempting to reflood the marshes so the Marsh Arabs can return to their original home.

The Ma'dan use reeds that grow up to 20 feet (six meters) high to build their homes.

Kurdish way of life

Many Kurds live in cities, where they work as teachers, doctors, government employees, merchants, and laborers. Others live in villages led by tribal chiefs called *aghas*. Village homes are usually made of mud brick or stone. Most Kurds in these areas farm and raise livestock. Some Kurds still live the semi-nomadic lifestyle of their **ancestors**, herding sheep and goats. They spend their winters in villages near the base of the Zagros Mountains, then move higher up the mountains in the spring to let their animals graze on the lush vegetation fed by the melting snow and rain.

The Bedouin

The Bedouin were once nomadic Arabs who traveled the ancient land of Mesopotamia searching for water and pasture for their camels, sheep, and goats. They lived in tents woven from goats' hair. Today, a few Bedouin live a traditional nomadic lifestyle, while others have settled in cities or farming villages. Their rich tradition of poetry, music, and folklore continues to inspire Iraqi culture.

Kurds

More than four million Kurds live in Iraq, mostly in the northern and northeastern Kurdish Autonomous Region. The region, also known as Iraqi Kurdistan, was set aside in 1974 so that Kurds could rule over local matters, although the Kurdish government is still ultimately responsible to the government of Iraq. The official language of the area, Kurdish, is related to the Persian language. Most Kurds are Sunni Muslims, and many practice Sufism as well. Sufism is a **mystical** form of Islam whose followers seek to unite with Allah through **reflection**, music, and poetry.

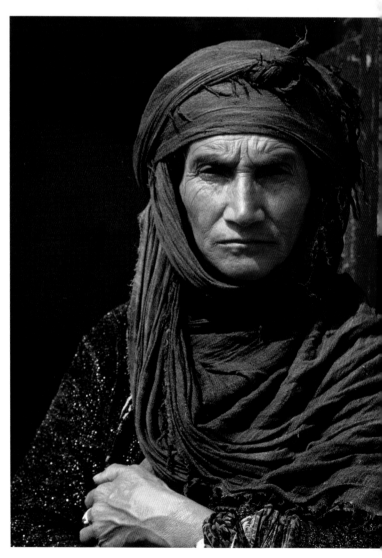

The two main Kurdish dialects are Kurdi and Kermanji. Kurds in Iraq understand both dialects.

Yezidis welcome the arrival of a peacock statue to their village. The bronze statue, shaped like a bird, is believed to give religious leaders divine power.

Assyrians

About 180,000 Assyrians live in Iraq, particularly in the northwest, which is their traditional homeland. They are the descendants of the Assyrians who established an empire in Mesopotamia from 1200 to 612 B.C. Assyrians speak Syriac, a language based on the ancient Aramaic language. Most Assyrians in Iraq follow a branch of Christianity called the Christian Nestorian Church, while the Chaldean branch of Assyrians belong to the Roman Catholic Church. One day each summer, Iraq's Assyrian community celebrates Nusardil, a joyful water-splashing festival that symbolizes the **baptism** of Jesus Christ and his disciples, or most loyal followers.

Yezidis

In northwestern Iraq, near the city of Mosul, live the Yezidis, who make up five percent of Iraq's Kurdish population. Yezidis' religious beliefs include elements of Christianity, Islam, **Zoroastrianism**, and **paganism**. The Yezidis' chief divine figure is called Malak Taus, the peacock angel.

Yezidis have been persecuted and tortured for refusing to convert, or change their religion, to Islam. Between 1640 and 1910, at least 20 massacres were aimed at extinguishing the Yezidi way of life. Today, they are no longer persecuted, but their faith is often criticized by non-Yezidis.

Turkmen

The Turkmen first entered northern Mesopotamia when Tamerlane invaded in the 1400s. Today, they are the third-largest ethnic group in Iraq. Traditionally, Turkmen were herders and expert carpet weavers who lived in villages and communities in the countryside. Many Turkmen now live in Iraq's cities in the north and northeast, especially in and around the city of Kirkuk. They follow the religion of Islam, speak a Turkic language called Turkmen, and have their own newspapers, radio stations, athletic clubs, and schools.

Two young Turkmen join a group calling for greater recognition of Turkmen's political and cultural rights.

Armenians

The Armenians are a Christian people who first came to Iraq in ancient times as traders from Turkey. Large numbers of Armenians also arrived from Turkey in the 1600s, when new rulers forced them to move to Iraq as traders, and in the 1800s, when they were persecuted. About 10,000 Armenians live in Baghdad, and another 10,000 live in towns and other cities across the country. They speak Armenian and follow either the Armenian branch of the Roman Catholic Church or the Armenian Apostolic (Orthodox) Church.

Mandaeans

The Mandaeans are followers of an ancient religion that developed in the first century A.D. They are often referred to as Sabians, meaning baptizers, or followers of St. John the Baptist. St. John the Baptist was a prophet who preached the word of God. In the 600s, after growing opposition by Muslim invaders, the Mandaeans moved from the cities of Mesopotamia to the southern marshes, where they lived for hundreds of years. In the mid-1900s, they moved back to the cities, especially to Baghdad, Basra, and Nasiriya. Those who still live in the marshlands continue their lifestyle as boat builders. Many other Mandaeans work as gold- and silversmiths, doctors, engineers, and teachers.

Millions of Iraqis have fled their homeland, either because of harsh treatment by the government or for economic reasons. Five million Iraqis now live throughout the Middle East, the Americas, and Europe. This woman and her child live in San Francisco.

Persians

Persians are Shia Muslims who come from the land east of Iraq. Their ancestors settled in ancient Mesopotamia after Cyrus the Great invaded the region in 529 B.C. Today, most Iraqi Persians live around holy cities, such as Najaf, Karbala, and Samarra, where important Shi'i religious leaders are buried. There are far fewer Iraqi Persians than there once were since many returned to Iran after the Iran-Iraq War. Many of those who remained have been absorbed into Iraqi culture. Those who have retained their Persian identity live as merchants in Iraq's cities, or as religious leaders in Najaf and Karbala.

Mandaeans take part in a baptism ceremony on the banks of the Tigris River in Baghdad. Mandaeans practice ritual baptism because they believe that running water gives life.

Country life, city life

Most of Iraq's people live in large cities. The rest of the population lives in the countryside, either in riverside villages, the northern mountains and foothills, or the desert.

Life in rural areas

Villages are often made up of several families that belong to the same tribe, which means that they share the same ancestry. Tribes have been part of Iraqi society since ancient Mesopotamia. Some of today's tribes trace their ancestors back to the first Arabs in Iraq. A sheikh, or *agha* in the case of the Kurds, is in charge of the tribe. The sheikh makes political decisions and often helps prominent families arrange marriages and settle family disputes.

Country and city homes

Villagers live in homes made of mud bricks with roofs made of straw. Hollow wind towers called *badgirs* stand on the roofs, sending cool breezes down into the homes. Wheat, barley, apples, pomegranates, lemons, beans, and eggplants thrive in surrounding fields.

People in cities live in apartment buildings or in houses made of cement, brick, or stone. Roofs are usually flat — the perfect place for hanging laundry to dry or for sleeping on hot summer nights. Some parts of the cities have large, new homes where wealthier families live.

Mud and straw houses in an Iraqi village.

A woman wearing an abaya selects eggs at a market in Baghdad.

Clothing

People in Iraq wear different styles of clothing depending on where they live and the lifestyle they lead. Many people in cities wear pants, shirts, skirts, and dresses very similar to those worn in North America.

Plain, long, light-colored dresses are part of women's traditional dress in many rural areas. Women and older girls from traditional families, both in rural areas and cities, wear headscarfs and long, dark cloaks called *abayas* over their clothing. Wealthier women wear *abayas* decorated with gold thread, fringes, or wide belts encrusted with jewels.

A traditional item of clothing for men is a *thobe*, which is an ankle-length robe with long sleeves. Summer *thobes* are made of light cotton, and winter *thobes* are made of wool. Men also wear turbans, which are pieces of cloth wound around the head, and *kufiyas*, which are scarfs draped over the head and wrapped with cord. These coverings protect the head and neck from the blazing sun.

Markets

People in villages and cities shop in markets called *souks*. *Souks* are especially busy in the evenings, when temperatures are cooler and more comfortable for shopping. Vendors in *souks* sell everything from clothing and housewares to fruit and gold. In large cities, there are different *souks* for different goods and services. For example, there are carpet *souks*, silver *souks*, and even doctor and dentist *souks*.

Having fun

Iraq's landscape provides its people with many opportunities to enjoy the outdoors. Iraqis fish, swim, row, and canoe on the Tigris and Euphrates Rivers. In the northern mountains, they hunt game, such as rabbits and birds. In cities, people go to see plays, movies, and concerts. They also visit with friends or spend time at home watching television, playing board games such as chess and backgammon, and listening to classical or popular Iraqi music. In villages, people often gather at the local coffee house to relax, exchange news, and conduct business.

Sports

Soccer is the most popular sport in Iraq. Not only does Iraq have a national soccer team, but every neighborhood in Iraq has its own soccer team, too. Men and boys of all ages take to the streets and alleyways to participate in the neighborhood games. Women and girls play soccer as well, and they participate in track and field and volleyball. Iraqis also enjoy basketball, boxing, weight lifting, horseback riding, and horse races.

A member of Iraq's Olympic soccer team gets tangled up with a Costa Rican player.

Life after war and sanctions

Life in Iraq has been severely affected by fighting and economic sanctions. Many buildings have been destroyed or badly damaged and unemployment is high. There is little money for food and other necessities. Everyday items such as books, shoes, and light bulbs can be hard to find. There are also shortages of gasoline, electricity, and clean drinking water.

The situation in Iraq is beginning to improve. Cities and villages are being repaired; newer technologies, such as the Internet, are being used in the country; and, since Saddam Hussein's government was overthrown, people have been able to share their ideas in conversation, as well as in the media, without fear of being punished.

Bombed and burnt buildings are visible throughout downtown Baghdad.

More than 2,000 years ago, traders came from India and Persia to Mesopotamia bearing spices such as cinnamon, nutmeg, cloves, cardamom, cumin, and ginger. The riches of the ancient spice routes still inspire Iraqi cooking.

All kinds of beans and spices are available for sale at Iraqi souks.

Women gather around mats for an outdoor meal on a warm, sunny day.

Breakfast, lunch, and dinner

Iraqis often begin their day with a breakfast of bread covered with thick cream and a date syrup called *dibis*. Eggs, potatoes, and tea, Iraqis' favorite drink, are also part of breakfast. Lunch, the main meal, usually includes rice and a hearty stew, roast, or kebabs of lamb, beef, goat, poultry, or fish. These meats are considered *halal*, or lawful, according to the *Qur'an*. Pork is *haram*, or forbidden.

Dinner is a light meal, such as fried eggplant, watermelon, and bread. A simple tossed salad of whole herbs is also common, as are leftovers from lunchtime.

House specialties

Iraqis enjoy *kibbeh*, which are small dumplings filled with minced lamb or beef, nuts, raisins, and spices, and *quzi,* a whole lamb stuffed with rice, almonds, raisins, and spices. *Dolma* is another popular Iraqi dish, made by stuffing a mixture of rice, raisins, meat, and parsley into grape leaves or hollowed-out vegetables, such as tomatoes, zucchinis, or peppers. Once stuffed, the *dolma* are simmered in a pot over a fire.

The most famous Iraqi dish is *mazgouf*, a fish dish made of carp from the Tigris River. The carp is cut open and lightly smoked over a charcoal fire, then stuffed with peppers, spices, onions, and tomatoes. It is grilled, skin down, on the fire's red-hot ashes, and a sauce is poured on top.

(below) Mazgouf is grilled over an open fire. According to tradition, only men are allowed to prepare this special dish.

(above) A woman prepares bread dough by rolling it out with a rolling pin.

Bread

Iraqis eat many types of bread. *Khubuz* is a flatbread that Iraqis dip in stews or wrap around meats. *Samoon* is a white, crusty bread. Most village homes and some city homes have mud brick ovens, called *tanours*, in which Iraqis bake bread over wood fires.

Regional cooking

Kurds eat many dishes made from northern ingredients. Lamb or chicken kebabs are served at many meals, but grilled partridge and quail flavored with wild herbs and mushrooms are also popular. Homemade yogurt sweetened with grape syrup and honey is another favorite treat.

A main dish of the Ma'dan is a yogurt mixed with rice and dates. The Ma'dan also hunt and eat waterfowl and fish, and enjoy a soup made with broth and beans.

What you need:
1/2 cup (125 ml) butter or margarine
1 cup (250 ml) white flour
2 cups (500 ml) chopped pitted dates
1 tablespoon (15 ml) anise seeds
1/2 teaspoon (2.5 ml) cardamom powder
sesame seeds, crushed walnuts or almonds,
sugar (optional)

What to do:
1. Melt the butter in a medium-sized pot or pan over medium-low heat.

2. Gradually mix in the flour. The mixture should turn a golden color. Be careful not to burn it.

3. Add the dates. Over low heat, gently mash them, and mix until all ingredients are blended.

4. Remove the date mixture from the heat. Add the anise seeds and cardamom. Mix well, and allow the mixture to cool.

5. Roll small portions of the date mixture in your hands to form one- or two-inch (2.5- or 5-centimeter) balls. Roll in sesame seeds, crushed walnuts or almonds, or sugar, if desired.

Ma'dan breakfasts are accompanied by a crisp, tasty bread that is baked in a clay oven.

Desserts

In the Middle East, many people believe that sweet things sweeten life and drive away sadness. Pastries filled with cream and dusted with powdered sugar, preserves, and honey are popular Iraqi desserts. *Zlabiya* is a sweet pastry that looks like a pretzel. The crunchy dough is dipped in syrup. *Halva* is a treat made with ground almonds or sesame seeds and honey. The mixture is baked in a pan, cut into squares, and topped with cinnamon or powdered sugar. Iraqis also enjoy dates as a sweet treat.

Klecha

On special occasions, Iraqis eat date balls, called *klecha*, for dessert. You can make *klecha* with an adult's help. The dates should be brown and soft. If they are tough, first toss them in butter over medium heat.

A pastry shop in Mosul is filled with tempting Iraqi desserts.

🕌 Off to school 🕌

Schools, or *madrasas*, in Iraq are free of charge for students attending kindergarten through college and university. Under Saddam Hussein, parents paid a fine if their children did not finish secondary school. In tougher economic times, however, many parents sent their children to work rather than school, so they could earn money for the family.

In first-level madrasas, courses are taught in Arabic, except in the Kurdish north, where students are taught in both Arabic and Kurdish.

Public education suffered during Hussein's rule. Economic sanctions resulted in a shortage of books and overcrowding. Some parents now choose to pay for their children to attend private schools.

First-level *madrasas*

Children begin kindergarten at the age of four, and first level, or primary school, at the age of six. Boys and girls attend primary school together. Children take classes in math, religion, drama, and language. After fifth grade, they begin to learn English and French. Students also have physical education every day, and many join school sports teams.

Students attend school either in the morning or in the afternoon. Having two shifts allows schools to accommodate large numbers of students. In wealthier areas, children attend school all day and have a longer break for lunch.

Children's games

Before and after school, Iraqi children like to play tag, hide and seek, marbles, and *tuki*, which is similar to hopscotch. Jacks, played with a ball and crystal beads, is another favorite game, as are Seven Stones and Stick and Robin. In Seven Stones, one team stacks seven flat stones to form a tower. A member of the opposite team throws a stone to try to scatter the tower, then runs between two points as many times as possible before the other team rebuilds its tower. Stick and Robin is similar to baseball, but the batter hits a short, curved stick instead of a ball.

Children enjoy jumping rope when they are not in class.

Second-level *madrasas*

At the end of first level, children must pass a standard national test covering all their courses in order to go on to second level, or secondary school. Boys and girls attend second level separately.

The first three years of secondary school are spent studying math, arts, science, and the history and politics of Iraq. The next three years are spent either in preparatory schools, where students get ready for college or university, or in vocational schools, where they learn a trade, such as carpentry or mechanics. Students in all schools must pass an exam at the end of second level to graduate.

College and university

Students who complete second level either enter the working world or attend university, technical college, or teacher training. There are eight universities in Iraq: four in Baghdad, and one each in Sulaimaniya, Basra, Arbil, and Mosul. There are also special universities that offer degrees in religious studies.

Mustansiriya University in Baghdad is one of the oldest schools in the world, dating back almost 800 years. The university has about 30,000 students, including many from other countries.

Nasreen was tired when she woke up in the morning. After a breakfast of eggs, potatoes, and tea, she helped her mother clean up.

"Why do you look so tired, Nasreen?" her mother asked.

"I couldn't sleep last night," Nasreen replied. "I kept thinking about Father's wonderful find at the site."

Nasreen's father, who was an archaeologist, laughed a little from the living room. "It's nice that you're so interested in my work. Maybe I could bring you along one day to have a look." Nasreen smiled.

Nasreen left for school early with her two older brothers. She pulled her *abaya* tight against the harsh wind. Her brothers held their arms up in front of their faces. The sand blowing in the wind made it difficult to see.

Nasreen, who was ten years old, attended first-level *madrasa*. Her older brothers were in second level. Nasreen couldn't wait to tell the class about her father's discovery.

When it was sharing time, Nasreen stood up in front of the class and explained, "My father is

Nasreen waits intently for the chance to share her father's discovery with the class.

an archaeologist. He's working at the ancient Babylonian city of Borsippa, south of Baghdad. Yesterday, he found a food container stamped with a name and date. It's almost four thousand years old."

"How did people long ago stamp a name onto a container?" her teacher, Mr. Abudallah, inquired.

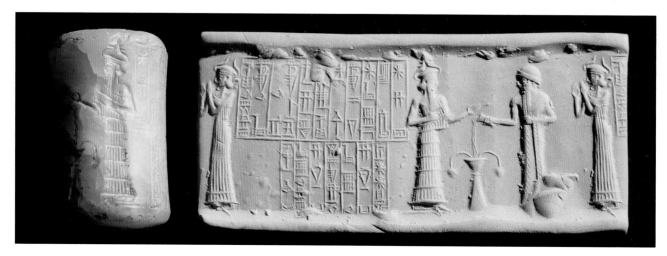

Each person's cylinder seal was carved with its own design.

Nasreen's father is among the archaeologists digging in Borsippa.

"They used a cylinder seal. It was a long, narrow stone with a carving on it. When they rolled the seal over wet clay, it left a permanent imprint."

"Why do you think people did that?" the teacher continued.

Nasreen answered, "To mark property as their own. Kings even stamped bricks with their name and the date. That way, everyone knew which palaces and **mosques** they had built, and when."

One of the children in the classroom put up his hand. "Yes, Kazem?" Nasreen asked. She liked pretending to be the teacher. When she grew up, she hoped to teach in a classroom just like this one.

"Does the food container belong to an ancient king?" Kazem asked.

"My father thinks it belonged to a merchant. My father also found other pottery and bricks buried in the dirt," Nasreen answered.

"A brick from a palace would be interesting, but pottery from a merchant's house isn't very exciting. Who cares about that?" asked Kazem.

"Lots of people do. It's important to learn not only about how kings and wealthy people lived thousands of years ago, but about how families and children like you and me lived," Nasreen answered.

The teacher stepped forward and thanked Nasreen for speaking to the class. Nasreen sat down at her desk, happy that she had shared the news of her father's discovery and proud that she lived in a country with such a rich history.

On her way home from school, Nasreen passes a souk where vendors sell dates from a wagon.

# Glossary

activist A person who works to change other people's ideas and actions about an important cause

allied Joined in a close relationship, as in one country helping another during a war

ancestor A person from whom one is descended

baptism A ceremony that welcomes a person to the Christian Church. During the ceremony, the person is dipped or washed in water, as a sign of washing away sin.

biological Related to living organisms

canal A manmade waterway

cease-fire An agreement between two countries to stop fighting and discuss peace

coalition A temporary political union for a particular purpose

coup The overthrow of a government

descendant A person who can trace his or her family roots to a certain family or group

dynasty A family or group of rulers that stays in power for a long time

economic Related to a country's system of organizing and managing its businesses, industries, and money

empire A group of countries or territories under one ruler or government

ethnic Describing groups with the same nationality, customs, religion, or race

fertility The capacity to grow, as with plants, or have children

illiteracy An inability to read and write

Islam A religion based on the teachings of Allah, the Arabic word for God, and his prophet Muhammad

mosque A Muslim house of worship

Muslim A person who follows the religion of Islam

mystical Spiritual

natural resource A material found in nature, such as oil, coal, minerals, or timber

nuclear Related to energy formed when atoms join or split

paganism A belief in spirits in nature

persecution The act of harming another person for religious, racial, or political reasons

profit Money kept after all business costs are paid

prophet A person believed to deliver messages from God

radical Having extreme ideas or beliefs

refinery A factory where natural resources are purified

reflection Careful thought

refugee A person who is forced to leave his or her home because of danger

Socialist Following an economic system where the country's natural resources, businesses, industry, and politics are controlled by the whole community

terrorist A person who uses violence to intimidate society or government

treaty A formal agreement signed by two or more countries

ziggurat A pyramid-like tower with a temple on top

Zoroastrianism A religion developed in ancient Iran by the prophet Zoroaster. It is based on the belief that a god who represents good continually fights with one who represents evil.

 # Index